HELLO, BODY!

HEART

by Joyce Markovics

 CHERRY LAKE PRESS
Ann Arbor, Michigan

CHERRY LAKE PRESS

Published in the United States of America by Cherry Lake Publishing Group
Ann Arbor, Michigan
www.cherrylakepublishing.com

Reading Adviser: Beth Walker Gambro, MS Ed., Reading Consultant, Yorkville, IL
Content Advisers: Sharon Markovics, MD, and Peter Markovics, MD
Book Designer: Ed Morgan

Photo Credits: freepik.com, 4; freepik.com, 5; freepik.com, 6–7; freepik.com, 8; © ilusmedical/
Shutterstock, 9 top; freepik.com, 9 bottom; freepik.com, 10; freepik.com, 11 left; © Jose Luis Calvo/
Shutterstock, 11 right; © TATLE/Shutterstock, 12; freepik.com, 13; © Shidlovski/Shutterstock, 14;
freepik.com, 15; © studiovin/Shutterstock, 16; © Captain Wang/Shutterstock, 17; freepik.com, 18;
freepik.com, 19; © Tatjana Baibakova/Shutterstock, 21.

Cherry Lake Press is an imprint of Cherry Lake Publishing Group.

Library of Congress Cataloging-in-Publication Data

Names: Markovics, Joyce L., author.
Title: Heart / by Joyce Markovics.
Description: Ann Arbor, Michigan : Cherry Lake Publishing, [2023] | Series:
    Hello, body! | Includes bibliographical references and index. |
    Audience: Grades 4-6
Identifiers: LCCN 2022003697 (print) | LCCN 2022003698 (ebook) | ISBN
    9781668909607 (hardcover) | ISBN 9781668911204 (paperback) | ISBN
    9781668914380 (pdf) | ISBN 9781668912799 (ebook)
Subjects: LCSH: Heart—Juvenile literature.
Classification: LCC QP111.6 .M36 2023 (print) | LCC QP111.6 (ebook) | DDC
    612.1/7—dc23/eng/20220224
LC record available at https://lccn.loc.gov/2022003697
LC ebook record available at https://lccn.loc.gov/2022003698

Printed in the United States of America by
Corporate Graphics

CONTENTS

A BROKEN HEART

Baby Fae's new heart thumped in her tiny chest. Her heart, however, was not the one she was born with. It belonged to a baboon! How did a human baby end up with a monkey's heart?

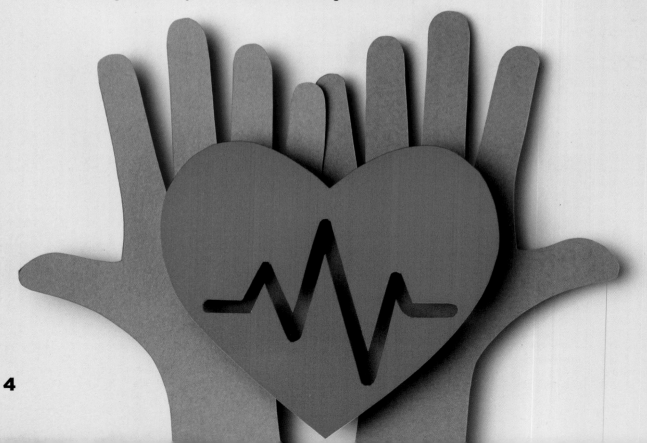

On October 14, 1984, Fae was born with a deadly **defect**. The left side of her heart was not fully developed. The **infant** was only expected to live a couple of weeks. That's when doctor Leonard Bailey, a heart **transplant** specialist, stepped in.

Humans and baboons are closely related. They share 94 percent of their DNA.

5

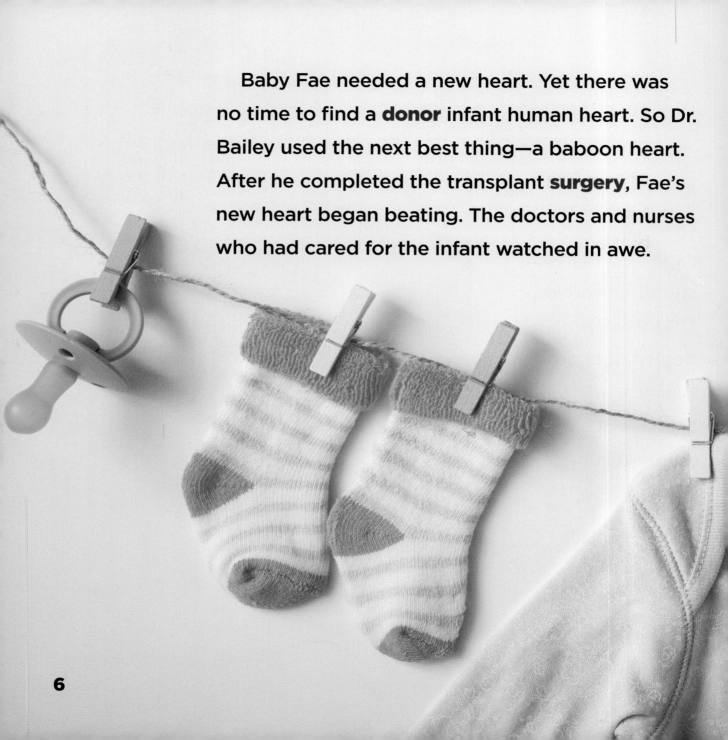

Baby Fae needed a new heart. Yet there was no time to find a **donor** infant human heart. So Dr. Bailey used the next best thing—a baboon heart. After he completed the transplant **surgery**, Fae's new heart began beating. The doctors and nurses who had cared for the infant watched in awe.

Fae lived with her new baboon heart for 21 days. Then she **mysteriously** became ill and died. However, Fae had lived longer than any baby with a transplanted heart—human or baboon. Dr. Bailey learned much from Fae. Later, he went on to successfully transplant human hearts in 376 babies!

The day after Fae's death, Dr. Bailey said, "Infants with heart disease yet to be born will someday have the opportunity to live, thanks to the courage of this infant."

GOT HEART?

Hold up your fist. That's about how big your heart is. Your heart is a small **organ** with a big job. Think of it as a pump made from **muscle**. Your heart sends, or pumps, blood around your body. The movement of blood is called circulation (sur-kyoo-LAY-shun). Blood gives your body the oxygen and **nutrients** it needs and carries away waste.

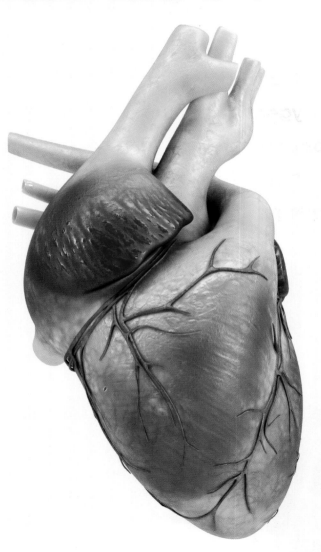

The heart has two sides. The right side of the heart receives blood from the body. This blood then gets pumped to the lungs, where it picks up oxygen. The left side does the opposite. It gets oxygen-rich blood from the lungs and pumps it to the body.

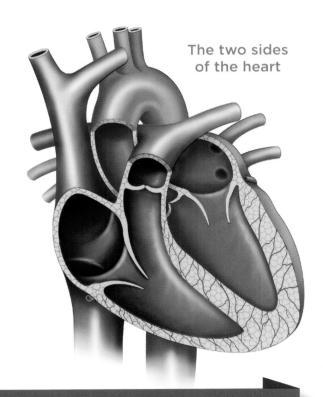

The two sides of the heart

People used to think emotions came from the heart. Nope! They come from the brain, which also controls the heart.

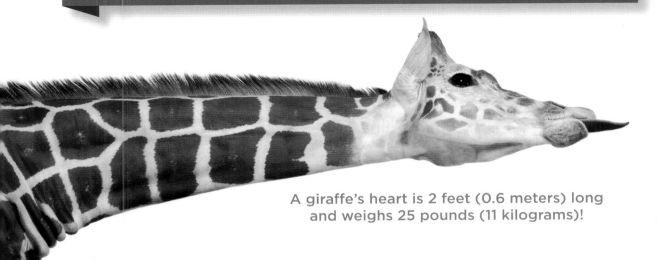

A giraffe's heart is 2 feet (0.6 meters) long and weighs 25 pounds (11 kilograms)!

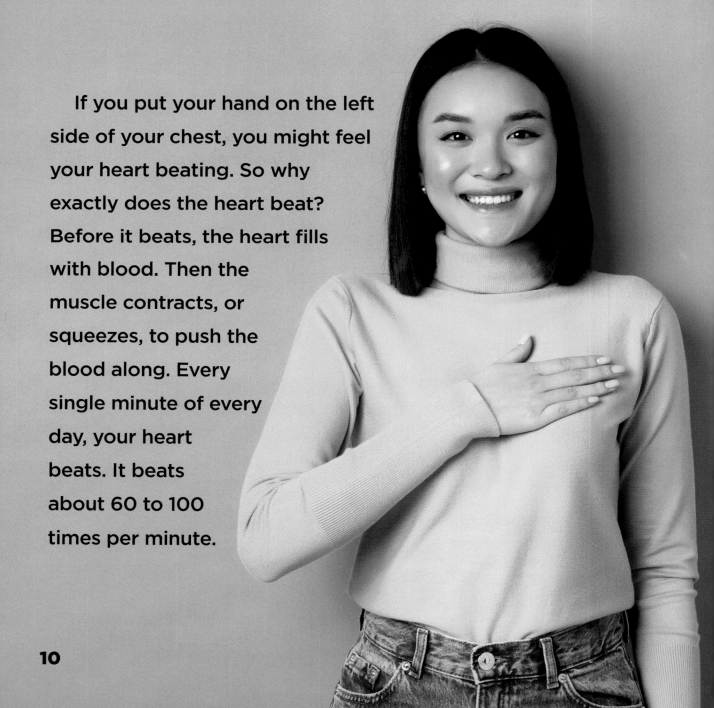

If you put your hand on the left side of your chest, you might feel your heart beating. So why exactly does the heart beat? Before it beats, the heart fills with blood. Then the muscle contracts, or squeezes, to push the blood along. Every single minute of every day, your heart beats. It beats about 60 to 100 times per minute.

The cells that make up heart muscle also beat! If you looked at one heart cell under a powerful **microscope**, you would see it pulsing. Think of it this way. If one heart cell is like a singer in a chorus, then your heart is like the entire chorus!

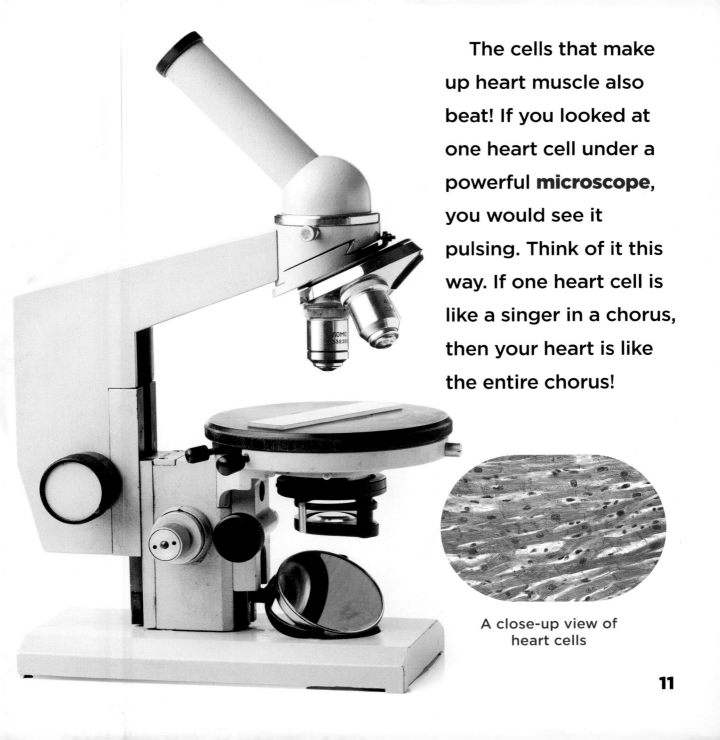

A close-up view of heart cells

HEART PARTS

The heart is made up of four areas, or chambers. Each side of the heart has two chambers. There are two on the top and two on the bottom. The top two chambers of the heart are the atria (AY-tree-uh). They receive blood. The bottom two chambers are the ventricles (VEN-trih-kulz). Ventricles push blood out of your heart to your body and lungs.

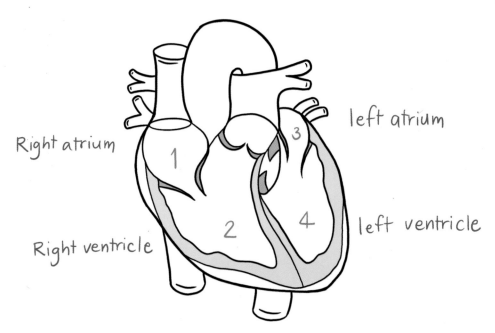

Right atrium

1

left atrium

3

Right ventricle

2

4

left ventricle

Here are the four chambers of the heart, including the ventricles and the atria. One atria is called an atrium.

The atria and ventricles work together. The atria dump blood into the ventricles. Then the ventricles squeeze the blood out of the heart. The atria refill, and the process starts all over again.

The human heart weighs about as much as two baseballs!

A thick wall of muscle, known as the septum, separates the left and right sides of the heart.

The atria and ventricles are separated by valves. Valves direct the flow of the blood. Imagine a door that swings only in one direction. That's similar to how a valve inside your body works.

This doctor points to an image of a heart valve.

The heart has four valves. Each one has a special name and job. Two valves—the mitral (MY-trul) and tricuspid (try-KUS-pid)—allow blood to flow from the atria to the ventricles. The other two—the aortic (ay-OR-tik) and pulmonary (PUL-muh-ner-ee)—control the flow of blood leaving the heart.

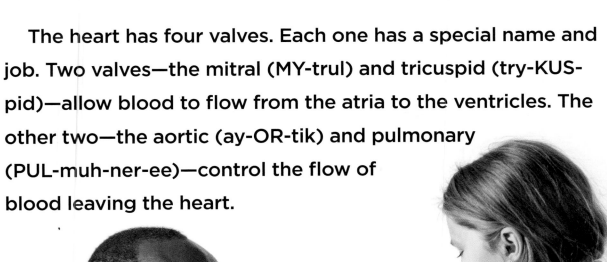
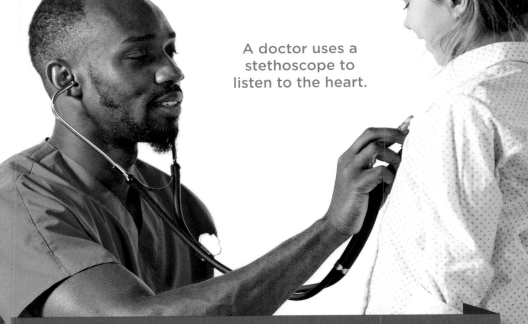

A doctor uses a stethoscope to listen to the heart.

If you had a stethoscope to listen to your heart, it might sound like: *Lub-dub, lub-dub*. That's the sound of your valves shutting inside your heart!

CIRCULATING BLOOD

Blood doesn't just slosh around inside your body like water in a bottle. It travels through blood vessels. There are three main kinds: arteries, veins, and capillaries (KAH-puh-ler-eez). In all, your body has about 60,000 miles (96,561 kilometers) of blood vessels. That's long enough to circle the globe twice!

The network of blood vessels in the body forms a loop, or a circle.

Blood vessels connect to the heart. Arteries carry blood away from the heart. And veins carry blood back to the heart. The two largest blood vessels are the aorta (an artery) and the vena cava (a vein). It takes your body less than 1 minute to pump blood to all your cells.

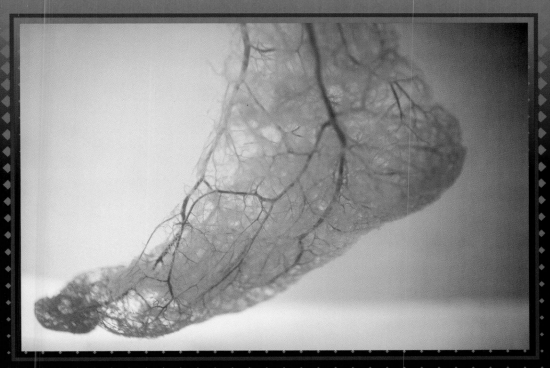

This image shows blood vessels in a foot. The thin, branching vessels are the capillaries.

Capillaries are your body's tiniest blood vessels. They branch all over the body and are thinner than a human hair.

One of the most important things your blood carries is oxygen. Each cell in your body needs it! Without enough oxygen, a person can't live. Blood picks up oxygen in the lungs. Then the oxygen-rich blood travels to the left side of the heart. From there, it's pumped to the rest of the body.

Blood is alive! It contains red blood cells that carry oxygen. This image shows what the cells look like.

Blood carries oxygen all the way to your fingers and toes—and to every single cell! In the process, your cells create waste, including carbon dioxide. As the blood circulates back to the heart, this waste is partly removed from the blood by your **kidneys**.

HEART TROUBLE

Sometimes, the heart doesn't work as it should. A problem called high blood pressure causes your heart to work extra hard. This can lead to heart failure. Also, as people age, their arteries can thicken. Hard paste called plaque (PLAK) can block the flow of blood in the heart. This can lead to a heart attack.

A heart attack occurs when oxygen-rich blood can't reach the heart muscle. Then heart cells may die. If the heart attack is severe enough, the person may not survive. But all hope is not lost. Exercise builds heart strength. And a healthy diet can help keep your heart healthy throughout your life!

Eating lots of vegetables and fruits helps keep your heart healthy.

Here are some ways to keep your heart healthy:

- Your heart is a muscle that needs exercise. Keep it strong by exercising at least three times a week. Walk, play, bike, jump, or dance.

- Maintain a healthy weight. Eat lots of healthy foods, such as vegetables, fruits, and whole grains. And avoid sugary drinks such as soda and fruit juice.

- Don't smoke! Smoking can damage your heart and blood vessels. And it doubles your risk of having a heart attack.

GLOSSARY

defect (DEE-fekt) an imperfection

DNA (DEE EN AY) the molecule that carries the genetic blueprint for a living thing

donor (DOH-nuhr) a person who provides an organ for another person

infant (IN-fuhnt) a very young child

kidneys (KID-neez) body parts that remove waste from the blood and turn it into urine

microscope (MYE-kruh-skope) a tool used to see things that are very tiny

muscle (MUH-suhl) a bundle of tissue in the body that produces movement

mysteriously (mi-STEER-ee-uhs-lee) in a way that's difficult to understand or explain

nutrients (NOO-tree-uhnts) substances needed by the body to grow and stay healthy

organ (OR-guhn) a body part that does a particular job

stethoscope (STEH-thuh-skope) a tool used to listen to a person's heart and lungs

surgery (SUHR-juh-ree) an operation that treats injuries or diseases by fixing or removing body parts

transplant (trans-PLANT) to take a body part from one person and place it in another

FIND OUT MORE

BOOKS

Simon, Seymour. *The Heart*. New York, NY: HarperCollins, 2006.

Simon, Seymour. *The Human Body*. New York, NY: HarperCollins, 2008.

Storad, Conrad J. *Your Circulatory System*. Minneapolis, MN: Lerner Publications, 2013.

WEBSITES

Britannica Kids: The Heart
https://kids.britannica.com/kids/article/heart/353235

The Franklin Institute: The Giant Heart
https://www.fi.edu/exhibit/giant-heart

National Geographic Kids: The Truth About Your Heart
https://kids.nationalgeographic.com/science/article/the-truth-about-your-heart

INDEX

ABOUT THE AUTHOR

Joyce Markovics has written hundreds of books for kids. She marvels at the human body—and all the things we still don't know about it. Joyce dedicates this book to her father, Frank, who recently had his heart rebuilt by a team of talented surgeons.